T0131606

It's All About *Love*

My Journey Back to I Am

KAY MCINNES

BALBOA.
PRESS
A DIVISION OF HAY HOUSE

Balboa Press books may be ordered through booksellers or by contacting:

Balboa Press
A Division of Hay House
1663 Liberty Drive
Bloomington, IN 47403
www.balboapress.com.au
1 (877) 407-4847

Because of the dynamic nature of the Internet, any web addresses or
links contained in this book may have changed since publication and
may no longer be valid. The views expressed in this work are solely those
of the author and do not necessarily reflect the views of the publisher,
and the publisher hereby disclaims any responsibility for them.

The author of this book does not dispense medical advice or prescribe
the use of any technique as a form of treatment for physical, emotional,
or medical problems without the advice of a physician, either directly
or indirectly. The intent of the author is only to offer information
of a general nature to help you in your quest for emotional and
spiritual well-being. In the event you use any of the information in
this book for yourself, which is your constitutional right, the author
and the publisher assume no responsibility for your actions.

Any people depicted in stock imagery provided by Thinkstock are
models, and such images are being used for illustrative purposes only.
Certain stock imagery © Thinkstock.

Print information available on the last page.

ISBN: 978-1-5043-1014-7 (sc)
ISBN: 978-1-5043-1013-0 (e)

Balboa Press rev. date: 10/02/2017

I dedicate this book to my daughter **Michelle**
*A child of the Universe who returned
home to Source on 11th April 2011,
without whose help this book would
never have been written.*

Preface

This book is about my spiritual journey and my truths that I learned along the way. I had never thought of writing a book like this until I had a reading with a lady called Ricci-Jane Adams PhD., the author of "Spiritually Fierce". During the reading she informed me that my deceased daughter, Michelle, was with us and she wanted me to write a book. My immediate reply was "about what?" She went on to tell me that I would know when the time was right to begin the book and it was to be aimed at younger people, and that Michelle would help me.

I must admit, that I left this reading doubting that this would happen. However, several months later I started writing in notebooks. The first piece that I wrote was actually the first chapter of this book. I continued writing whenever I felt directed and before long I had 2 notebooks with many writings on different subjects. Then one day I just decided that I should start putting my book together and was quite surprised to find that I had about half a book and that all the pieces just seemed to fit together one after the other, so I continued to write.

Having lost 2 adult children, I found that some of the chapters that I was writing were indeed therapy for me, and as I wrote I began to understand myself and my soul much more clearly. So, thank you Ricci-Jane and Michelle for getting me started.

(Throughout this book I have referred to Source, The Universe and God, which are all different names for the same. If you are not comfortable with any of these please substitute whichever one feels right for you.)

Chapter 1

Life isn't fair. But what is fair, who judges? It is all about beliefs and conditioning. If we believe that life isn't fair, then that is what it will be.

There are always reasons for what we perceive as unfair, it may be a lesson we have to learn or it may just be something which needs to happen in order for our true path to be revealed or followed. Why? is a question we ask continually from childhood. But to get the answer we have to pay attention to the NOW in our lives and listen very carefully. There are many ways to receive these answers – it may come as a sudden idea in your head, it may be something that somebody says to you, it may be in a song or in a book that you are reading, or it may be something that you see and suddenly a light goes on.

True answers always come with love – if something is true for you, you will always feel the love in it as it comes to you, in whatever form that may be.

There is no easy or quick way to get from where you are to where you are meant to be. It is a step by step process and many of these steps are very difficult and teach us hard lessons, but as long as you learn from these and do not give up because life is too hard, you are on the right path for you.

Many people would say that my life has been very hard, and it certainly has contained many losses. However, without each one of these I would not have come to where I am today, or indeed be the person that I have become.

Love is the key and this has to be learnt, the first step being to learn to love yourself. And if you can truly do this then the rest is easy. This is a universal Love - no judgements, no conditions apply to it and once you can love yourself in this way then it will naturally extend to all things and you will find this true love coming back to you as well. Many people search for years, looking for that one person or thing to make them happy, not realising that it is all within us and all we need to do is access the divine love within.

I was not born into a spiritual family and always felt a little lost or out of place, as I was intuitive from a reasonably young age. There was always an interest in all things spiritual, but because I had no-one to teach me (or rather remind me) what I really already knew in my soul, I was reluctant to just throw myself in the deep end. So it took me until my 60s before I was ready to walk the spiritual path. The catalysts for this were actually tragic occurrences in my family. In the end there was no further down that I could go – so I needed to find a new direction, to save my life and my sanity.

It seemed that my life had been a series of challenges and my human side told me that I needed to find answers from outside myself. My ego told me that I just needed someone to fix it for me, or if I just had more money or time or help then everything would be fine. But I now know that this is not the case. If the answer doesn't come from within then it will only fix the problem for a short time and then it will be back, or some other challenge will take its place. It seems to me that the more we have, the more we think we need in order to be happy, when all the time we already have everything we could possibly need, we just have to look within and find it for ourselves.

Every challenge in this life is an opportunity to learn a lesson and evolve. If we do not take up this opportunity it will be presented to us again at a later time. Therefore, some souls are able to evolve quicker than others. If we can approach a challenge with love, we are already on the road to turning the challenge into an opportunity to promote our evolution and learn the truth of who we are and fulfil our life's purpose. The evolution of spiritual awareness does not stop. No matter how far you have come there is always more.

You may have memories from your childhood of seeing, hearing or sensing angelic beings, beings of light or departed loved ones. However, if you were like me, you were told that it was a dream or your imagination and so you eventually believed this and the veil between you and the spirit world became more solid and caused you to forget who you are and where you came from. Your ego took over and created the life it wanted for you, and so the struggle that was never meant to be, began. A life of separation that was not real, although the ego made this life appear to be the only reality. But there is no separation – there never was and never will be, in reality there is only Oneness.

Chapter 2

E very challenge which you may, at the time, view as a disaster, is really part of the big picture, which we can't yet see. It may take time, but eventually the reason will fall into place. It may be necessary for you to experience great loss or sadness before you realise your life's purpose – why you have come to the Earth plane in this lifetime. While many people do go through loss and grief and have many life challenges to deal with in order to realise their life's purpose it is possible to do it without these crisis events.

You have probably already completed some of your tasks without even knowing what they were. I was the mum of 3 children, and like all mothers tried to do the best I could to bring them up to be responsible adults. There were times when life seemed good and at other times it seemed to be a struggle. Then they were grown and had children of their own, though they never ceased to be my children.

So when my eldest son, at age 26, was diagnosed with an inoperable brain tumour, here was one of the greatest challenges for our family. He passed away just before his 31st birthday, but in that last 4 and a half years he taught us many lessons by just being the person that he was, and letting his beautiful soul shine through his human frailty. Though he was going through this terrible illness, he was always concerned with how the rest of us were doing. Only a week or two before his death he said to me "Are you and Dad worrying about me kicking the bucket?" I replied to him "we don't want that to happen, but whatever happens, we will deal with it and we'll be OK."

By the time of his passing, it was a relief to me, because I did not want him to go through any more suffering. We had been blessed in so many ways having him in our lives, but it was time for him to go. Though to those of us left behind there was a big hole in our lives which felt as though it would never be healed. Maybe we were being prepared for another loss.

Less than 10 years later, on 11th April 2011, my youngest child, Michelle, suicided at the age of 31 years. In the years before her death she suffered from a lot of depression and other undiagnosed ill health. Less than 2 months before her passing she was actually diagnosed with Borderline Personality Disorder with Conversion Disorder. At the time of her passing, she had 2 daughters aged 12 and 3. This tragedy started a series of incidents which saw me spiral to the depths of despair.

It wasn't until a book called "Healing Grief" by James Van Praagh, came into my hands that I began to make my way back to normal. I feel that this book was sent to me by Michelle, and then many more were to follow.

I became interested in anything spiritual and I know I was looking for my lost daughter. I discovered a meditation group and became a regular attendee, sure that Michelle would appear, but instead I found my true self.

As I had always been interested in healing, I did a Gift of Light Healing Course, and started practicing what I had learnt.

Over the years since Michelle's passing I have read many books on spiritual subjects – most of these I am sure have been sent to me at the right time. Many spiritual teachers believe that when the student is ready the teacher will appear, and most of my teachers have been books, which have just turned up in my life when I have had questions in a certain area. These books just seem to answer and clarify whatever it may be that I am struggling with at the time. If you are a reader, which I have always been, then this will be an easy and natural way to learn. Others may need personal one-on-one or group sessions to be stimulated into looking within for the answers you seek. Because they are all there, we just need to learn how to look within and tap into all the wisdom and knowledge that each being has from many lifetimes, or simply from Source.

Over the last few years I have done several courses and workshops conducted by Angelique Adams of Lightworker Training and also her daughter Rici-Jane Adams PhD through her Institute for Intuitive Intelligence. Each one of these that I have attended has given me much inspiration and clarification with regard to my spiritual journey and the direction which I needed to follow at that time. I received many benefits because I resonated with both Angelique and Ricci-Jane and to me their teachings were true and gave me a path to follow. In fact much of what they taught I already knew, but didn't remember that I knew it until they reminded me. There are many such teachers all over the world, so if you find one that resonates with you, then give yourself permission to take the opportunity to learn whatever it is that you need to learn.

Chapter 3

Loved ones in spirit can, and will, communicate with those still on the Earth plane. However, you must give permission for this communication, and it can come through in many different ways. You may get direct communication from someone in spirit, although more often it will come through a third person, or, you may hear the answer to a question in a song or read it in a book. I have a son and a daughter in spirit and they have both communicated with me through a friend of mine who is a medium. Though there are times when I do get messages direct, these are usually in dreams or during meditation.

Recently passed souls appear to be very good at interfering with electrical or electronic equipment to let you know they are OK. While I was using my Dad's computer to write a Eulogy for his funeral service the computer would freeze in the middle of something and then the screen would go white and the computer would turn itself off. I believe that this was my Dad letting me know that he was supervising what I was doing. I have used his computer several times since and it has behaved perfectly.

Many communications are very subtle and we must

pay attention or we could miss a message, as we have no control over the way such messages are sent to us. Very often it is a time and place and method that we are really not expecting. Souls in spirit often show their presence by a feather or a coin, so look out for those.

I was recently at a Country Music Festival and felt sure that Michelle would appear there, as she was a country singer and song-writer. I thought maybe a feather, as this had happened in the past, but no. It wasn't until one of the artists, who was performing, was talking about a song that he had written and he was telling the story of how it came about, that the feather came through. There is an eastern belief that when you pass on, your heart is weighed against a feather and the hope is for your heart to be lighter than the feather. Here was my feather – not even remotely what I had expected.

Some souls are very good at communicating while others find it very difficult, and some even have to relay their messages in order to get them to the Earth plane. However they come, they are always sent with Love.

After my daughter passed away I went searching for her. I thought if I did spiritual workshops and went to meditation groups she would appear. But instead I discovered my spiritual self – I found, not her, but the I that I am. Once I became comfortable with this, she did start to come through to me in many ways at the times when it was right.

Through a meditation group I met a friend who is a medium, and after a while Michelle started contacting me through her. As my spiritual journey progressed I was able to have direct contact with her in meditation, and some of my healing clients had messages for me from her. I needed to learn how to listen, as many contacts are very subtle and not usually in the way you would expect.

A couple of years ago I had the strong feeling that my daughter, Michelle, wanted to write a letter to her daughter, who was then 17. After a week or so, and this feeling just kept coming up, I finally sat down with pen and paper and said "OK write!" The letter that emerged was beautifully said and I gave it to my granddaughter, explaining how it came about.

As much of this letter is true for everyone, I have included it here in this book with my granddaughter's permission.

Letter From a Mother in Spirit

Dear Daughter,

> *I know I left you long before you wanted me to go and you felt that I was not there for the many times in your growing-up years when you felt that you needed me and missed me so much. But let me tell you that I was with you every step of the way, encouraging and comforting you so that you would make the decisions that were for your highest good. Many times I was so proud of your achievements, some of these were great, others only small, but you made a difference in some way to yourself and others.*

I know that life has, and will throw you many challenges, and the way that you react to and handle these challenges will influence the direction of your life. As long as you feel the love in all that you do you will be going in the right direction for you at that time in your life. If you do not feel love in a decision you are making, think it through again and see if an alternative may feel better for you. Though it is your life and your path and you, (as I did with mine) are the only one who can walk it and you must choose your way. There will be times when you feel overwhelmed and at these times just sit and breathe and ask for assistance or guidance, and if you drop your consciousness into your heart the answers that you seek will come. It may not be immediate, and it may not be in a way that you expect, but just be aware of subtle signs and messages, and you will just know what you are meant to do for your highest good.

I know that you will not always take this direction, as sometimes your ego self is just too persuasive. I know, because I have been there, and sometimes the path to where you need to be can be very rocky and take many twists and turns which may not have been necessary if you had made some different choices.

Remember, that I am always near you and am always sending you love and light. The love I had for you on the earth plane has not gone away, it has just changed slightly and is now pure spirit, but nevertheless still so very strong.

I see the many challenges you face and it would be wonderful to just put them all right, but each spirit who has chosen to come into human form must walk the human path, as was destined before their birth.

I will love you forever, and there will always be a part of me alive in your heart and this is why you are so like me in many ways.

Your loving Mum.

Chapter 4

Happiness is yours to choose. Relying on other people or things to make you happy does not work. True, you may feel happiness and pleasure for a short time, but any happiness which does not come from within will not last. It took me many years to discover the truth of real happiness.

You think to yourself, if I just have a new car, house, etc. I will be happy or maybe it's someone to share your life. The only thing you can rely on to make and keep you happy is your own soul – you must choose joy and happiness and let it come from within. This is the only happiness which can last. You may know someone who always seems happy, and when they are around you, you feel happy too. It comes from a peace deep within their soul which they are truly connected to in a way that allows them to find the joy and the good in every situation, no matter what it may be. It may feel like they are filled with light, which shines out into the world. Whether or not they realise it, they have chosen to allow the Divine part of themselves to shine through the human body, which they are using in this lifetime.

When you find true happiness within yourself then

other people and things, which may improve your life, will be attracted to you, but they are not <u>necessary</u> for you to remain happy. If you have the attitude that they are nice and you enjoy them and are grateful for them, but you do not <u>need</u> them, your life will be in flow and peace, and the struggle will be gone.

Learn to love yourself unconditionally, with no judgements or fears that you won't measure up. Change the way you think about yourself. Instead of telling yourself "I am not loveable", "I'm too fat, too unattractive, too weak, too old, too young, etc. change your thoughts to "I am loveable, I am attractive, I am young, strong, just the right weight, etc. and I truly love myself."

Just having these beliefs about yourself will make them true and you become comfortable with who you are so that it is not necessary to have someone to keep telling you these things (which you don't believe anyway), as you know them yourself.

Believe in yourself, trust that those things that you intuitively know are true, and will lead you along the path that you are meant to walk. I have learnt that you cannot rely on another person to lead you in the right direction. You must make your own choices and have faith that the things that feel filled with love are right for you. You can receive inspiration and clarification from others, but in the end it is you that has to make the choices and walk the walk.

When I first started on my spiritual journey I thought that I should have a teacher who would tell me all the steps I needed to take, but I soon learned that this was not the way of it at all. I felt let down. I felt like I had a certain amount of instruction and then was left to my own devices, thrown in the deep end so to speak. I thought "how am I going to get to the next part if no-one will show me the way". Then slowly I realised that I had to do it myself, my way, and though I felt that I didn't know what I was doing, as nobody had actually told me, I just started doing the things that it felt right to do whenever a situation or opportunity arose. Before long I was running a meditation group and my healing sessions always felt filled with love. Both my client and I felt comfortable with the sessions and the outcomes. When talking with my clients about their experiences I discovered that they were confirming the things that were coming up for me during the session. I didn't need step by step instructions once I had the basics, but simply to follow my intuition at all times.

As long as I am living from the love and happiness inside of myself and relying only on what I already have within, to be happy and at peace, then every aspect of my life will reflect that peace and happiness. What we feel inside we project into the world and it is mirrored back to us by people and events, so that what we give out, we ultimately receive back.

You are not a victim. The only person who can make you a victim is you! You are the creator or your own destiny. In order for you to be a victim of anything, you yourself must accept what your ego is telling you and believe that because of whatever has happened you have been wronged. But it is only in your mind, because if you refuse to feel victimised and make the situation into an opportunity to grow, then there will be a completely different outcome.

Most of my life I have blamed circumstances, occurrences or other people for my bad luck. And especially after my daughter's passing, I felt that I was a victim of life and circumstances. I wanted to know "why have these things happened to me, what have I done to deserve this." I was really in a "poor little me" state, not knowing which way to turn or what to do to get out of this situation. As a victim, I thought that there was nothing that I could do by myself to change my life and all the terrible things that just kept happening to me.

It was only when I got to rock bottom and feeling that life was not worth living, that I came to realise that I had to do something myself to have a life that was acceptable to me. I had to reject the feeling of being a victim, because if I acted that way, that is how others would treat me, which didn't help me at all.

Maybe I was lucky with some of the professionals who were treating me, because they were able to help me turn my thinking around, rather than just prescribe medication to block it all out. I remember one psychiatrist who I saw around this time saying to me "you do need some medication to get you on the right track, but it is only a mild dose". But he also suggested to me that things like regular exercise would improve my mental health. So I started walking most days and doing acquarobics, and realised that they did indeed make me feel better. I also had a psychologist who had spiritual beliefs and she encouraged me to explore by spiritual side and try things like meditation.

So, slowly, step by step my thoughts of being a victim changed, and I came to a place where I could choose to be happy. Though it didn't really feel like I was happy at first, but as I chose to see joy and goodness in things and people, what I was seeing and feeling started to change and people began treating me in a different way.

I also met others who were on similar journeys, people who had also had losses in their lives, and we were able to support each other. (I also met people who were not ready or willing to accept support at this time and without their permission, whatever support we could offer them was not helpful to them. They had to take the first step and be open to accepting change and whatever assistance was available.)

Those of us who were ready for change were able to help each other. Together we learnt to have gratitude for what we had in both the present and the past and not dwell on the grief and sadness, which had previously consumed us. We no longer felt sorry for ourselves because we were victims, but felt that there were reasons for living, and joy and happiness were possible if we looked inside ourselves.

I am not saying that I am now completely happy and peaceful all of the time. There are times when I fall back into being a victim, or feel sadness or anger, but I now know that I can turn these feelings around and life can be better. I am the one who has to make the first move to bring about change.

There are ways that you can bring yourself back to balance and peace. Find something that you really enjoy doing, something that calms your soul and makes your heart sing. It may be swimming in the sea or walking on the beach or pottering in the garden. It may even be something as simple as sitting on a rock and contemplating the sun sparkle on the water or the wind blowing through the trees. It may be going for a ride on a horse or a bike. It may be something else entirely, but it is the one thing that makes you come alive. Once you have found what this activity, or non-activity is, do it as often as you can. It may be necessary to actually make the time for this special thing, but the benefits will be very worthwhile, and your soul will thank you.

Chapter 5

Choices are made, either from fear or love, or in other words, from the ego or from the higher self.

To choose to forgive someone or something is just the first step. Though you may be willing to forgive yourself and/or others, there is more to it than that and it could take quite a long time for this process to be complete.

I am amazed at what lengths that some people will go to control others. Mostly, it is not even because of what another person is doing, but more likely just the fear of what they may or can do at some point.

Some years ago I had a problem with a family member who perceived me as a threat and took all sorts of actions to prevent me from doing something that I desperately wanted to do. My reactions were from a place of fear and I grieved for something that I feared I would never have again so I developed very strong feelings against this person.

It was some time before I began to realise that nothing in this situation would improve until I had forgiven him and myself, but how to go about this was quite beyond me at first. I did not think there could be a time when I could think of him or speak of him without feeling the anger and the hate.

I started sending him love, though at first it didn't feel real, but over the months and years I would think of his good points. And I had come to understand that he had just been acting from the perspective of fear, so the blame I had felt began to diminish as I consciously released negative thoughts. I could then allow my thoughts and feelings to come from a place of love (higher-self), rather than a place of fear (ego).

Almost 4 years later I realised that the anger and hate were no longer there when I thought of him. I had forgiven myself and him. There is still a long way to go, but we are at last moving in the right direction to heal ourselves and the situation.

Forgiveness is not instant and in some cases there is a lot of work and releasing to be done before there is a result. You actually need to get to a place where you can feel the love for yourself and the other person in order to release and forgive. If you ask for and are willing to accept assistance from the spiritual realm to release the fear and change it to love, forgiveness is possible in even the most complicated and seemingly impossible situations.

Chapter 6

Fear is a very human trait presented to us by the ego in its endeavours to control us. I know, like most people, I spent a very large part of my life being fearful of many things. I was always afraid that bad things would happen or that situations would not work out the way I wanted them to, causing me to spend many hours worrying about this fear. My human mind just went round and round trying to make sure that none of these fears came true. However, it did no good, because the more I worried and tried to work it out the more fears would raise their heads. It always seemed that my life was just going from one crisis to another. It was not until I changed the fear to love and acceptance that my whole way of thinking became one of being in the flow, instead of being a constant struggle, wondering all the time what the next crisis would be and how I would deal with it.

When you live from a place of fear it is like you are walking a tight-rope and your emotions are so wound up that it is like a spring just waiting to break. Whatever we think about is what the Universe delivers to us. So thinking about what you don't want gives us more of that, because the Universe does not recognise negative or positive, the only message it receives is the subject of the thought. So saying to yourself "I don't want this headache any more" will just bring you more headaches.

One of the greatest fears most people have is fear of death.

It is my belief that the death of the body is not an ending, but in fact, a beginning of the next stage of life. At what we perceive as death, the spirit or soul is set free from the earthly limitations of the body. The life in the body has been a learning experience to evolve the soul on its way to its full potential.

Life is eternal and without the limits and restrictions of the body the spirit is free to return to true oneness, without the ego trying to organise, restrict and change the true nature of the spirit to fit into the human perceptions of life.

I believe that once our body has died, we are then free of all the beliefs and restrictions and conditioning that we have received here on earth.

My father was of the belief that once you die that is it – you just go to sleep and there is nothing else. However, the night after his death he came to my sister and said to her "I was wrong, you don't just go to sleep."

But because the human mind cannot understand concepts which it has not seen or does not know about, it is very difficult for most of us not to be sceptical about what happens at death. Many people, my husband included, say that no-one has come back to tell them what it is like, so there is nothing once we are dead. They are not willing to believe or trust in what they have not seen. Even though there are many documented instances of near death experiences, where a person has actually died and come back to life and described the continuation of the soul, this seems far beyond the human comprehension of some people, so it is unacceptable to them. They cannot see the air we breathe, but they do know and accept that it is there and is keeping our body alive. And because we have accepted this concept, we are aware of breathing the air in and we can actually feel it entering our body through our nose.

Maybe one day the concept of eternal life will be accepted just the way the breath of life is accepted. This is a part of the evolution of human consciousness, so that humanity, as a whole, can raise its' vibrations and return to the truth of love, which has been forgotten, as the ego drew humanity away from their true nature with its promises of adventure and excitement. These promises were, of course, not truly delivered. Sure there may have been experiences of this adventure and excitement, but it did not last and did not bring happiness or peace of a lasting kind.

Chapter 7

Writing can be a great therapy in times of stress and troubles, but also in good times. If you write down every day what you are thinking and how you are feeling, you will be creating some coping strategies for your life. In writing all the sad, frustrating, angry, disappointing, stressful thoughts and feelings you are releasing them from your being. Once you have written these thoughts and feelings in detail you no longer have to go over and over them in your mind. And if you write down all your thoughts and feelings which are loving, happy, pleasant, contented, accepting and filled with excitement, then when your thoughts and feelings are not good you can read over these and hopefully, change your perceptions, thus turning around your thoughts and feelings.

Keeping a written record of your thoughts and feelings allows you to see just how far you have come on your journey. You may be feeling that life is very bad at the moment, but if you can look back on your thoughts and feeling of maybe 6 months ago you may realise that things are not as bad as you think and have actually improved significantly.

When I look back on bits that I wrote 2 years ago or 3

years ago, I realise exactly how far I have come on my path over this time. I also realise that I don't go backwards. Yes, there may be new challenges but I have learnt new and better ways to work through them, so that I am always going forward, even if it sometimes doesn't feel like it. There are still times when something will happen and I lose it, but these times are further apart and not as intense as they have been in the past.

I have been told that for me, writing is a type of meditation and I have come to realise that this is indeed true. If I have questions, I write them down and then continue writing and the answer will come. In fact, most of this book has been written in exactly this way, with a word or a phrase coming into my mind and then I sit down and write about it.

My daughter was a singer and she wrote many songs, some of which we are lucky enough to have recorded, so if we feel inclined we can have her sing to us, even though she is no longer here in the flesh. When she was writing songs she would often ring me and sing to me over the phone, a song she had just written. It was a privilege to be a part of this process. One day after she had been writing songs, she said to me:

"Mum, where does all this come from. How do I know the words, I don't even think about it, it just flows. I stop and read what's written and even though at times it doesn't make sense, I swap some lines around and a masterpiece is in the making."

She was just following her intuition and writing from her heart.

As I write this book I am feeling much the same,

because the words just flow and when I read back what I have written, I too have no idea where it has come from.

Not long ago, I woke in the middle of the night with the words to a song going around in my head, but it was nothing I had ever heard before and I felt compelled to get up and write in down. When I read it back in the morning I realised that it was beautiful and very appropriate for the world at this time.

Without Love

Without Love the world is sad,
Without Love the world is empty,
Without Love the world is fear,
Without Love the world's not here.

So draw the Love from Mother Earth's depths.
And from the Heavens above,
So that the world will be peace, joy and love.

Share the love and heal the world,
Share the love and fill the world with Light,
Share the love and dissolve the fear,
Share the love and make it right.

Now I just need someone to write the music and really make it into a song.

Chapter 8

Meditation is increasingly becoming part of many people's daily life. Many traditional doctors and health workers now believe that meditation is beneficial for their patients for maintaining good health, both of the body and the mind and also the spirit.

Meditation takes many forms. It is a tool to quiet the mind so that you can go within to find the inner peace whereby you find the balance, purpose and joy in your life, which cannot be found externally. We all have, in our Divine Soul, all that we need to make us happy, balanced and fulfilled – there is nothing outside our being that can truly do these things for us in a way that is ongoing.

The simplest form of meditation is just sitting quietly and breathing in and out and keeping your awareness purely on your breaths. You may place your awareness on a thought, a word (e.g. a chant) or an object, such as a candle or a flower, anything to take you away from the everyday grind. Think with your heart rather than your mind.

A walk in nature can be a meditation. As you walk, by just being in the NOW and noticing what is around you in each moment, you are meditating.

I have been told that my best form of meditation is writing. You do not have to know what you are writing, just take up a pen and begin writing whatever comes into your thoughts, or it may go straight to the page without your mind really being aware of what you are writing.

There are also guided meditations, where you are guided on an adventure which will be your own individual one. A number of people listening to the same guiding voice will meditate in different places and on different things. In meditation, whatever comes up for you is what you are in need of at that time. There is no right or wrong way to meditate, the main thing is just to do what feels right for you on a regular basis.

I hold a meditation group a couple of times a month and at first I was always amazed at how whatever was needed by those people in attendance was what came up during the meditation. Now I have just accepted that what is necessary, at the time, and in the lives of those present will occur in one way or another. It is all about tuning into the vibrational frequency necessary to receive whatever messages or knowledge are appropriate from the light of Source.

I spent a large part of my life feeling as though I was walking a tightrope, not knowing when I was going to fall off, or be pulled off. As this was my expectation, it happened frequently – I seemed to go from one crisis to another with maybe a little bit of joy and happiness in between.

But there was never any peace – I never felt at peace with myself. I was just trying to live to other people's expectations. First, my parents and siblings, and later, my husband and children were the ones who directed my life. I didn't know that all I needed was to love myself and find my own peace within my soul. And it took me many years of searching in the wrong places – outside of myself – expecting to find people or things or events which would give me this ingredient in my life which was missing, and allow me to find true happiness that would last.

It wasn't until I decided to explore my spiritual aspect, the Divine part of my being, that I began to find peace and joy and real love and light in my life. It had been there all along but my ego had persuaded me that I didn't need to go there and my ego self would provide whatever I needed. So getting in touch with my higher self was a very long and slow process. Although, once I had contact with this part of my being, I just wanted more because I could feel my truth. I had had glimpses in the past but did not allow myself to open up and receive that which is my Divine right. Allowing and accepting is a major part of being able to live from your higher self, and just knowing that every single thing that you need you already have within you is the first step.

Once you change the place that you are coming from, the world around you will change. When I was living from the ego many of the people around me were in need of something from me, and their friendship was not given in unconditional love, but only in order to get something from me that they felt they needed at the time. Whether it was help in doing something by using expertise which I may have had in a certain area, or needing me to nurture them in some way, they all wanted to use my energy to their advantage, without truly giving back to me. At that stage of my life I'm sure I was probably doing the same thing. I found that as I changed many of these friends simply dropped away.

I still serve others, but these days the people I attract around me always have gratitude, not that this is necessary to me, but in the receiving of what they need they are also giving. Their giving may even be in the form of a chain which goes around, whereby I have given them something they need and then they are able to do a service for, or give something to someone else – paying the love forward so to speak.

For many years I lived with stress and anxiety and had no idea how to access peace and calm. Much of the time I felt agitated, waiting for the next crisis to strike, and because I was expecting it, inevitably one would arrive. This was just confirming to me that my ego mind was right, and even when things seemed to be going well and life seemed good, I just knew that there was something ready to pounce and spoil it all. Since learning to meditate, I no longer get into this distressed state, or on the rare occasion when I do start to feel stress or anger, I sit quietly and pay attention to my breathing. I consciously breathe into my heart – breathing in love and light and breathing out love. Or it may be breathing in peace and breathing out calm – you can make it anything that works for you. After about 5 minutes of doing this simple exercise, I always feel calm and once again, in control.

It is very easy, in the troubled times we live in, to feel completely overwhelmed by life and feel that you will never get everything done or get where you need to be on time. If I do feel this at any time now, I just stop and say to myself, as I breathe gently, "there is plenty of time" or "I will arrive at just the right time". And funnily enough it always seems to be the case.

Chapter 9

If you have the belief that you are not able to raise your vibrations high enough to communicate with the highest beings of light then this will remain the case until you are able to let go of this belief. As we are all an aspect of God, we all have the ability to raise our vibrations to the highest levels. It may take much practice, but if we have beliefs blocking the path then it will not happen until these are released.

There can be a number of reasons for a person to have this belief, the most common one being that we do not think we are good enough or worthy. Life on this Earth can be very difficult and hard on us thus we may have perceptions about many things, none of which are strictly true, though at the time they may be true for us, as this is our perception.

This is where learning to love ourselves comes in again. Self- love and acceptance of the Divine being that we are will bring us to our truth. This truth is not the same for everyone, as it depends on exactly where each person is on the path back to their true Divinity. There is no right or wrong when it comes to truth, but you will know what is true for you, as it will truly feel right and will have a peaceful, loving feeling to it – it comes from the heart, not the mind.

When I am reading a book, especially if it is dealing with a subject that may be new to me, if it resonates with me I can accept that it is true, at least for me at the time. You will always feel the love in something that is your truth.

As I have learnt from reading many different authors, if you follow your heart and stay aligned with the Love which is within you, the universe will take care of the details. To me this seems to be very good advice to follow in life.

Chapter 10

I am a Lightworker. I do actually have a certificate which says I have done the training to be a "Light Work Practitioner". However, I believe it is much more than this. I know I can channel the light to my client when giving a Lightwork Session or healing, but this is just the technical part – the real light work is just allowing the light to shine from within, so that people you come into contact with will see it or feel it, and thus gain some benefit which they may be in need of at the time. Even if they are oblivious to this light, it can still work for them.

The Light is not limited, it doesn't run out – we can fill our heart with Light from Source whenever we wish. We just have to operate from our heart and not our mind, and give permission to receive the Light – it's as easy as breathing it in.

At this time the world needs more Lightworkers, to spread the Light into the areas where there is war and unrest and darkness in any form. Once you take light into a dark place, the darkness dissolves and there is only light. A group of people meditating on spreading the Light to where it is needed can do much to heal the world, because the Light they are working with is multiplied many times once it is sent out. Spreading Light can be as simple as doing a kindness for another person or animal, or just giving a smile to a stranger.

Just give permission for the Light, which is actually Love, to shine through you. If everyone did this then there would be no darkness. Whatever we give out always comes back to us, for in giving we are making room to receive.

You will find that once you start doing this people will come into your life that are on the same journey as you are, and sharing with them will make the path smoother and will give you confirmation that your direction is right for you at the time. Some of these people will be teachers to give you the next step. We need to have faith that each step added together will eventually form the whole picture.

The year after my daughter's passing, on waking one morning I had a vision of something like a gypsy camp with lots of coloured flags around, and all of a sudden it was as though a bright star shot into the scene. At first it gave me a start, but then I thought "oh no, it's just light shining". I had no idea what this was about until a few months later when we were attending a country music festival where Michelle used to sing.

At this venue there were always lots of stalls selling clothing, camping gear, etc., but this year there was a gypsy caravan, complete with colourful flags. This was the abode of Miss Gypsy Whitemoon, who was offering card readings. She also had Catherine Reynolds sharing her stall. Catherine was promoting and selling her book called "Invoking the Light", which I bought.

Because this was Michelle's territory, so to speak, and this type of stall had never been there before, I knew that there was something there for me. I thought maybe I should have a reading, but I later realised that Catherine's book was the light in my vision of a few months back.

This book was all about bringing the Light into your life and I now use the invocations in it every day.

This can be adapted to fill any situation with Light and it has now become an almost automatic part of my everyday life.

To my way of thinking if you are always in the Light there can be no darkness, because darkness is only the absence of light.

Chapter 11

You are not alone. Each of us has many spiritual helpers. All we need to do to access assistance is to ask and be grateful for what we have and what we receive.

I know when I can't find my keys for instance, and I am running around looking for them, if I just stop and ask "please show me where my keys are", I will find them. Then I always say thank-you to let them know that I am grateful for their help.

Some of these beings (although we may never see them) have been with us our whole life and others may change according to where we are and what we are doing in our life at any given time.

One morning after meditating I saw three or four small blue rings which were sparkling. I thanked them for showing themselves to me and asked "who are you." The answer I received was – We are all the higher parts of you, here to assist you in living this earthly life that is your purpose. You know us as different beings and we have changed although we are always the same and one with you and each other – we are aspects of your God-self and we are sending you love and light to help you do those things which it is your path to do."

I was very grateful for this insight that I had been given, as living on the earth plane is very difficult if you go against the flow of energy. But if you go with it and allow God to guide your life it will be much easier. Do not be attached to your ego self – do not allow it's persistence to influence your decisions, but follow the more subtle loving guidance of your higher self and its many parts.

Chapter 12

I have pondered why it has taken me so long to awaken to my spiritual self. "Why is this so?" I asked.

The answer that I have received is because I have needed all the experiences of my life to make me who I am and to enable me to have an understanding of the human virtues and frailties, so that I will fully understand what it is to be awake.

Apparently, I had many jobs to do in this life before I came back to the business of going home and knowing exactly what this means.

When I came into this life I had an agreement that I had to do all these other things to make me truly fit for my ultimate purpose in this lifetime, which is to be a teacher and healer.

In order to do this I must have first-hand experience of many human frailties in order to help others, even if it is just through reading something that I have written. I had to forget all the true knowledge that I have, so that the feelings and fears would be shown to me exactly as they would be for any person going through these challenges. This was so that I can truly understand many of life's challenging situations and the natural human reactions to them.

Chapter 13

I am often asked "how do you do it?", because I talk about my son and daughter who have passed as if they are on a holiday or out for the day. It wasn't always this way. I had to go through all the human grief processes before coming to a place where I am comfortable with how things are in this world. My whole way of looking at life has altered. Once I realised that we are a spiritual being in a human body and not a human body that has a spirit, my whole way of thinking changed.

It was going through this grief process which brought me to where I am now on my journey. This was one of the challenges of life which became an opportunity for growth and understanding. Since I was ready and willing to take this opportunity and make the most of it, and not wallow in the grief and loss, I found the path back to who I really am, and much more. As my thoughts and feelings turned from the ego perception towards the spiritual perception, I then became more accepting and comfortable with all that had happened in my life. I now remember all the good things and happy times with my departed children and do not dwell on unhappy times, though I can still speak of these if necessary. At these times I may feel a momentary sadness for <u>myself</u>, but I also feel happy because I know that they (my son and daughter) are now free and happy and will always be around me, even when I am not aware. I now choose joy and peace rather than sadness and torment.

It does take time though. There is no such thing as an instant fix. You can't wiggle your nose and suddenly you feel great and everything is wonderful. You have to go through all the steps and we can never see the end, just the next step.

From a place where I felt despair and there was no hope and I felt nothing would ever be good again, I am now at a good place filled with light and love. But it has taken me years to get here, and I didn't give up when it felt like I was going nowhere, just kept doing the next step, even when sometimes it was hard and I just felt like giving up. Somewhere deep down I knew that things would get better – one step at a time. Now I'm not saying that everything is now perfect – it's not, and can't be in this world, but whenever a challenge arises it is much easier to deal with. I now don't dwell on the bad things that happen (often this just makes them appear worse than they actually are). Problems just seem to resolve themselves without all the hassles and worry. It's as if the solution is just waiting there for the challenge to occur.

Recently, while parking my car, I hit the gutter with my front wheel, splitting the tyre. Of course it instantly went flat. As I got out of the car to check on the damage an angel of a man, who had watched the whole thing happen, immediately offered to change the tyre for me. I gratefully accepted his offer, and a situation which could have been a major hassle for me was resolved without my having to stress over it, trying to work out how to fix the problem.

Often things that happen in this world don't make any sense to our human brains. This is because we are thinking through our ego self.

When my daughter passed many people said "oh, what a waste of talent", as her songs and singing was one of the things that made her special and stand out. But as I've said before, this was part of a bigger picture, and once I'd been able to change my thinking from my ego to my heart, I was able to think about this differently. Sure, she was no longer here writing songs and singing and making beautiful music, but we can still play the songs she had recorded. These recorded songs are still affecting people who never met her in the flesh – she has left her legacy behind for the enjoyment of many.

And I believe she is still writing songs, though now she has to do it through other people. I have never written a song or poem in my life and yet the words I wrote down in the middle of the night are the words of a beautiful song - A true gift.

Chapter 14

Reading is one thing that I get a lot of joy from, and for me, books are one of my greatest teachers. I will read something in a book and it will ring true and then something else might trigger other thoughts and ideas. Some books I have read recently have inspired me to get on with the writing of this book.

They have made me think about my uniqueness and about many ways that I can share my soul and its wisdom with those who have ears ready to hear. It doesn't matter if it has already been said, there are many ways to say the same thing and different people resonate with different ways. Just let it out, as the more times and the more ways that the message is given, the stronger it gets and increases the light which spreads to the places and souls who need to wake up. Nothing is ever wasted if it is done with love.

From that dark place where I was only 5 years ago, it seemed that there was just no way out. I felt completely overwhelmed and that there was no hope for me to be happy or at peace.

However, though at the time I could not see how things would change, there was something inside of me urging me to go on. It took many sessions with counsellors and psychologists and support groups and a couple of trips to hospital, as well as psychiatrist treatment before I could even acknowledge to myself that my life was improving and that maybe there was a light at the end of the tunnel.

The only way I could go forward was to just look at the next step and not look at the whole picture, because that was way too scary and the whole thing just overwhelmed me. Before long I came to realise that I was indeed making progress. By paying attention to the now and looking within myself for answers, my thoughts were diverted from the past events and my ego's fears for the future.

And by just paying attention to the next step, I was progressing without even realising it until I looked back and saw how many steps on the path I had actually taken. It seemed that I was like a sponge, simply soaking up what I needed.

Chapter 15

I feel that my daughter made what some would call the ultimate sacrifice, so that I could walk the spiritual path that was always my purpose. Somehow life got in the way and took me far from my destined path and I needed to go through all the emotions of losing a son and daughter in order to get myself back on track. I had lost the love – the real love. Sure there was love in my life, but it was only superficial and did not last. It was the kind of love that needs material things and other people in order for it to be present and it never lasted very long.

I needed to wake up to my true nature and realise that I am a spiritual being having a human experience in a body and not a body which has a spirit. And it did take a long time to get to this realisation, step by step, working my way through all the ego driven falsehoods.

First I had to get to the very bottom, where the feelings of hopelessness made me feel that there was nothing left of any value, so I just had to find some new value in order to go on.

Then the books started arriving, each one at the perfect time, with the information that I was ready to accept.

Then, while the books were still coming, people began to appear who had more information and encouragement to add. And the path slowly began to form into a clear direction. At the same time those people who were actually opposed to my spiritual path or had no interest in it started to fall away, or if they did not, then their attitude began to change to fit more with the direction I was taking and these hindrances to my purpose were slowly but surely disappearing. I even found allies in places which in times past would never have existed. In changing my attitude and thoughts, those around me either began to change, or were just not there anymore.

On looking back, I see that one of the probable blocks in the way of my spiritual progress was my husband's views on spirituality. I thought that I needed to have the same beliefs as he did and it took me a long time to realise that even though we were married it was not necessary to think exactly the same way on every subject. Once I came to this realisation I started to follow my heart more, especially in regard to those things that I felt strongly about. But as I changed, subtly, so did he, allowing me to do those things I knew were on my path and in some instances, he actually promoted what I was doing, even though he did not understand what it was about, especially in regard to my healing work.

From an early age I was conditioned to believe that I needed approval as to the way I lived my life and the things I did. So no matter how strongly I felt I wanted, or needed to do something, if others disagreed and told me it was not the right thing to do, then most likely I didn't do it.

Over the years there were some things which I was determined to do, no matter what anyone else thought. These were those things which I felt in my heart were right for me at the time. (One of these was my marriage, and now 49 years later I am still happily married to the same man. Sure, we have had our ups and downs, but always come out the other side as strong as ever.)

However, most of the time I would fall in with what others wanted me to do. I didn't like confrontation and to me this was the only way that I could get others to approve of my choices. It was just easier to go along with what someone else thought I should do.

When I look back, I realise that the times when I was happiest, or felt the most joy, were those times when I did what I truly felt in my heart was right, whether it had approval from someone else or not.

Our main aim in this life is to be happy, so we either do those things which, in our heart, we know give us happiness, or we find happiness in what we are doing, no matter what it is or why we are doing it. The happiness is there within us, waiting to be claimed, we just have to make the choice.

Do not live your life for, or through other people. We all possess the full blueprints for our purpose in this lifetime – we just have to have the courage to remember it and then proceed in that direction, with or without those around us.

So make a difference and LET THE LIGHT OF **YOU** SHINE BRIGHT!

Printed in the United States
By Bookmasters